Wholesaling

A Beginner's Guide to
Wholesale Real Estate

By: Glenn Nora

Table of Contents

Furthermore, the information that can be found within the pages described forthwith shall be considered both accurate and truthful when it comes to the recounting of facts. As such, any use, correct or incorrect, of the provided information will render the Publisher free of responsibility as to the actions taken outside of their direct purview. Regardless, there are zero scenarios where the original author or the Publisher can be deemed liable in any fashion for any damages or hardships that may result from any of the information discussed herein.

Additionally, the information in the following pages is intended only for informational purposes and should thus be thought of as universal. As befitting its nature, it is presented without assurance regarding its prolonged validity or interim quality. Trademarks that are mentioned are done without written consent and can in no way be considered an endorsement from the trademark holder.

Introduction

Congratulations on purchasing *Wholesaling: A Beginner's Guide to Wholesale Real Estate*, and thank you for doing so.

The following chapters will discuss how you can make your breakthrough in the real estate investment industry by wholesaling. Don't worry if you are just a beginner because this book will start from the basics and give you a comprehensive idea of wholesaling. So, with this book, you will know what you are doing right from the beginning. And in today's world, real estate wholesaling is something that goes hand in hand with all the latest entry-level business strategies as well.

The wholesaling industry in real estate has a risk-averse nature, so if you want to get started in the industry, there is no better way than wholesaling as it will act as a stepping stone toward bigger ventures. In this book, you will not only learn what wholesaling of real estate is, but you will also get an overall idea about the benefits you can enjoy by venturing into this world. After you complete the book, you will have acquired a baseline knowledge, and this will get you started. As with any other business, even in wholesaling, the more prepared you are, the better it is for you because then you will be better prepared for the bumps on the road.

There are plenty of books on this subject on the market, so thanks again for choosing this one! Every effort was made to ensure it is full of as much useful information as possible.

Chapter 1: What Is Real Estate Wholesaling?

Real estate investments should not be compared to investing in bonds and stocks. It is true that you can get started with as little as a hundred dollars in these two types of markets. Also, you can enter the market whenever you feel like it, and you can exit at your own will as well. But when it comes to properties or estates, it is not so easy. Navigating through the world of real estate is really a tricky thing, and not being careful can often result in a hefty price to pay on your part. Also, selling and buying homes does not happen in the blink of an eye. It will take you days or even weeks. There are a lot of things involved in the process, like getting the right options for financing, doing all the extensive paperwork, and the matter of closing a sale. You still might want to make some profits in the world of real estate, but you might not be able to save up all the money required to deal with properties, don't worry. You still have some options open to you, one of which is real estate wholesaling.

You must know that real estate is a completely legal process that you can use to your advantage if you know the strategies. The best thing about this is you don't have to make any hefty down payments whatsoever.

Basics of Real Estate Wholesaling

One thing that you need to understand is that, with real estate wholesaling, you can make huge calculated profits. The most common misconception that people have about real estate wholesaling is that it is somehow related to retail wholesaling, but trust me, it's not! To clear your misconception, let's start with what retail wholesaling is. Here, quite a large quantity of goods is sold by the wholesaler to a retailer. The retailer is then responsible for repacking and then selling those goods to the consumers. They do this at a high price level. Since we are speaking about a large number of goods here, the amount that a wholesaler charges a retailer is quite lower.

When it comes to real estate wholesaling, it is not about selling multiple properties. In fact, it is a completely different scenario altogether. The wholesaler finds a seller and then contracts a home with them. Then, the next task of the wholesaler is to find the right buyer who might be interested in buying that property. The price that the wholesaler puts into a contract with the buyer is considerably higher than what he/she contracts with the seller. So, the difference in amount would be the wholesaler's profit. Usually, the distressed properties are the ones chosen by the wholesaler. But this is different from flipping because the wholesaler isn't really responsible for any renovations to the property and, thus, carries no costs.

So now, you must be wondering who should be getting into the wholesaling business. Well, it is mostly suitable for those who are beginners and looking for ways to get into the real estate market. This is also suitable for those who don't have the finances to invest in a business.

Flipping vs. Real Estate Wholesaling

It is important that you understand the difference between these two concepts. The fact that there is quite a lot of similarities between these two is why people often get confused between them. Looking at both, the property is required to make a profit by making it a means to invest. But both of them have some key differences, too.

For starters, flipping takes a much longer time than wholesaling. Thus, there is a difference in the time frame. Also, as already mentioned above, in wholesaling, the wholesaler will not be responsible for making any kind of repairs or renovations to the house. With flipping, you may go as far as renovating the whole house and add furniture to make it desirable to the buyers you want to attract.

Now, you must also understand that, in the case of real estate wholesaling, the risks associated are way lesser than flipping. The major reason being is that the wholesaler is not investing any money of his own. In flipping, many of the costs have to be taken on by they new investment owner, including property taxes, mortgage, insurance, and so on. Therefore, in terms of capital, flipping requires a lot more than wholesaling. But the success you will get in wholesaling purely depends on your market knowledge and also how good you are in making profitable connections because connections are what will fetch you better sales.

Who Can Be a Real Estate Wholesaler?

You might have a lot of questions in your mind regarding whether or not you can be a real estate wholesaler, but don't let your questions stop you from pursuing your goals. Basically, anyone can be a wholesaler in the world of real estate, but you also need to know that in order to be satisfied in this field of work, you need to be aware of three things on which your happiness and satisfaction will depend.

- **Have enough emotional support** — This is extremely important. You need to be in the association of entrepreneurs who are like-minded; otherwise, you can get emotionally depressed. If the people around you do not have similar goals in terms of finance and lifestyle, then it can impact you in a negative way. Also, it can become challenging when people you love or those around you start raining down on you based on the investment choices you have made.
- **Always take small steps** — You may have big dreams, and it is advisable to have them, but you should be setting up micro-goals toward that ultimate big dream. This will help you achieve your goals more efficiently without becoming overwhelmed.

- **Believe in the lifestyle you want** — You need to understand that wholesaling is all about making a huge chunk of money in a single transaction. You can make anything from $20,000 to $80,000 in a single deal, which is a lot harder to do in a 9-to-5 job. So, you need to spend some time brainstorming why you want to get started with wholesaling in the first place so that you get clarity on the fact whether it is for you or not.

Chapter 2: Major Benefits of Wholesaling Real Estate

As a start-up business, wholesaling of real estate property is much easier than other start-up businesses. In a real estate wholesaling business, the wholesaler acquires property from a seller at a discounted price by entering into a contract for reselling the property for a profit. A wholesaler must sell the property before the expiry of the contract with the original seller. This chapter will discuss the benefits of entering a wholesale business in the real estate industry.

1. **Easy Start-up**

   Wholesaling of real estate property does not need any licensing. It is also worth mentioning that wholesaling is not illegal. The only thing that you must comply with is the wholesaling law of the state where you make your deals. Therefore, you should be well informed about the law regarding the wholesaling of real estate property that governs the area you are interested in.

2. **Easy to Learn**

   You can easily grasp the basics of real estate wholesaling with a little effort. You only need to have basic knowledge of real estate and build from there. Discussions with other wholesalers who are working within the same district for more than five years will also help you effectively learn and efficiently handle multiple deals in a month.

3. **Easy Result and Easy Cash**
   Wholesaling of real estate, e.g., house property, provides you the advantage of faster payments. Sometimes, the cash is paid within the day, sometimes, even an hour.

4. **No Need for Cash or Credit**
   No cash or credit is required in wholesaling real estate property. When you are wholesaling real estate, you are not required to buy the property. All you need to do is sign a contract with the original owner of the property to sell that property to a buyer for a profit.

5. **Independent of Location**
   You might be wondering if you can choose any location in the world to deal with property transactions. Keep in mind, to begin wholesaling real estate, you should choose your preferred location where you can feel free to talk with the other wholesalers who are already working in the market. This will make you familiar with the market demand and the legal framework related to the wholesale in that region.

6. **Larger Market**
   It is a great idea to enter into the world of real estate wholesaling. Investors, banks, government, sellers, wholesalers, and buyers are all associated with the real estate world. Wholesaling is big business. So, there is a huge demand for a real estate property, and a huge demand protects your interest.

7. **Greater Experience**

   You will acquire great experience as you deal with real estate and enter deep into the industry. Once you learn the art of closing the deal, you will find different avenues for expanding your business, such as repair, renovation of the property, etc.

8. **Higher Income Opportunity**

   Income from wholesaling of real estate has no upper limit. However, your earnings vary on the type of property, size, and location of the property. Earnings also depend on the amount that investors charge on it. Despite all these, the income of wholesalers is higher than other property-related businesses, such as management fees, rentals, etc.

9. **Higher ROI**

   As a wholesaler, you can markup real estate by 5%, 15%, or 30%. You can also flip different house properties each month. Even if you invest your own cash, the return is much higher than the average returns from any other asset classes. If you have decided not to invest your money, your ROI will be even higher.

No Need for Property Listing

The property wholesaling business stands mainly on three pillars—a willing owner to sell the property, a wholesaler, and a willing buyer. Thus, wholesaling does not necessarily need to list the properties where the public has access to it. So, the real estate business involves the direct assignment of the contract. Using bird dogs in your real estate wholesaling will immensely help you in identifying potential and willing property sellers. Bird dogs are highly efficient in tracking down distressed properties. They do the job of a property finder and help to finalize the deal for which they charge fees.

10. No Membership Fees

A property wholesaler has no obligation to join any governing body or association; thus, a wholesaler does not have any legal requirement to pay any fee to any such body or association. Though a realtor has to pay the association's annual membership fee, the wholesalers are different from them.

11. Potential Volume of Business

The wholesale of real estate properties is a booming business worldwide. Rapid urbanization has added additional fuel to the system. This is because there is practically no limit in dealing with several properties that you can close in a month. Some wholesalers close a dozen deals in a month, whereas some close a half-dozen deals in a week. So, the wholesale of real estate has a huge potential volume.

12. Minimum Risk

There is no such business that is free of any risk. The risks in wholesaling of property arise only when you hold on to the same property beyond the due date. Under such a situation, you should seek out a willing and eager investor to make sure that your motive of "quick in-and-out closing of the deal" within the stipulated timeframe is achieved.

13. No Maintenance or Repair Costs

In the practical field of real estate wholesaling, every wholesaler keeps a ready list of buyers who keeps their capital ready to purchase distressed properties. These buyers, in general, are the real estate investors. They purchase, repair, and rehabilitate the properties at their own cost and take the risk of reselling those properties at a considerably higher price. So, as a wholesaler, you do not require to pay any sum for repair or maintenance.

Chapter 3: How Does Real Estate Wholesaling Work?

You might be asking yourself how much money a wholesaler can make a month from real estate wholesales. It ranges from $5,000 to $20,000 per deal, depending on the amount involved per transaction. If you can make at least five deals a month, you can easily earn at least $25,000 each month. However, it sounds great, but it's not an easy-going matter in the real world. Instead of looking at the potential earnings, you should focus on the working system of the real estate wholesale. This chapter will discuss seven different steps to deal with real estate wholesaling.

Find a Property for Wholesale

First things first, try to find out an absentee owner. You can earn more than the amount that you assign the contract for a property that belongs to an absentee owner. The ways to locate an absentee owner or a distressed property are discussed next:

- **Real Estate Wholesale Groups and Investment Groups**: There are several real estate wholesale and investment groups working under their umbrella. These network groups include real estate agents, contractors, title companies, and appraisers. These groups send emails out to their members every week, informing them of the details about the availability of different properties for sale. Take the opportunity to include yourself in such groups to take advantage of being associated with other wholesalers. By following group emails, you get to keep tabs on properties other wholesalers wish to buy and sell. You will understand the negotiation process and how much a wholesaler is selling a property for.

- **The Sites for Real Estate Wholesale**: This is another big place where you can find different distressed properties and specific types of properties you are searching for. You should utilize these sites to find out the prospective sellers who are willing to sell their properties immediately. To do so, you can visit particular sites, for example, HomesByOwner.com, FSBO, Craigslist, etc. While looking at these sites, you must put the city location where you are interested in searching for the distressed properties and you will also find the willing sellers. You can also use keyword search terms which you type into search engines to get better results. Such keywords may be:

  o Distressed property
  o Willing seller
  o Sold as-is
  o Estate sale
  o Must sell etc.

- **Hire a Professional Property Finder**: Another effective way to search for distressed properties and their motivated seller is to seek the help of a professional property finder. You can appoint a property finder within your real estate budget, which can assist you in finding prospective and interested sellers with whom you can make a deal. The professional you appoint as property finder may not necessarily be an employee of your firm but may be paid per deal of a property settlement.

Convince the Owner and Present an Offer

As soon as you find a distressed property, you should immediately sit down with the owner of the property to convince them to sell you that property and assign you the contract. This is the most important part of wholesaling the property and earning some profits. The following are the suggested steps that can help you to finalize the deal:

- **Keep Conversation with the Owner Courteously**: While approaching the owner, you need to create a credible environment for discussion, so that the owner can trust you for the property deal. For such a meeting, you can seek help from a professional. You should meet the owner on time, courteously, and with due diligence about the deal.

- **Present Your Offer to the Owner**: While proceeding in a negotiation with the owner, you should focus on the benefits that the owner can get from the seller's point of view. Some wholesaler focus on relieving the pain-points of possessing a distressed property. Some focus on the issue of legal formalities, such as the inspection of the property, appraisal of the property, and settlement of deal; these are things that an owner does not need to worry about. Some offer highlights that the owner is not required to pay any upfront charges.

However, you should explain to the owner about the all the repairing that needs to be worked on to get a prospective buyer. It is very important to convince the owner that the amount required for repairs will justify the price of the property.

- **Assignment of Contract**: Finally, there is a need to sign the contract. For this purpose, you should seek the help of an attorney who can guide you on the clauses which need to be included in the assignment of contract.

Find a Title Company, Appraiser, and Contractor

- An appraiser appraises the property and its value. He or she ensures that the price of the property that you agreed to pay is right and that you can make a profit from the wholesale of the property.

- A title company examines the legitimacy of the property and if it is free from any prior charges or encumbrances. They also help you to deal with the assigned contract of the property.

- A professional contractor is a ready person who can give you an appropriate estimate of the repair work necessary for the property. This will help you find a prospective buyer and make the right negotiation. However, as a wholesaler, you are not required to fix the property but sell it as is.

All these three types of professionals can be found from referrals of a wholesaler group.

Assessment of Needs for Property Renovation

Almost every property needs some renovation. Since the existing structure is the main foundation of the building, the rectification of defects in the structure, if any, has to be examined. Before doing renovations, an assessment of the existing structural design of the building is necessary to understand the scope of the renovation. The assessment will reduce the unnecessary involvement of costs on the renovation project.

A distressed property of an absentee owner, which requires a renovation, implies that you need to keep a higher margin while wholesaling the property to the investor. You can tell your contractor to estimate the costs likely to be involved in the renovation work. This estimation sheet will help you as a negotiating tool while talking with a prospective buyer. An investor will know about the renovation work that is needed for a particular distressed property and the involvement of cost therein; he or she will know the ARV (After Repair Value) of the property. You will be able to motivate the investor to buy the property; thus, you can earn a larger margin of profit.

Search for a Buyer

When you have found and acquired property to sell, you have all the professionals on hand to appraise the property, check the legitimacy of the property, and estimate repairs or renovation work needed for the property. So, you have everything in place that is necessary for a property wholesale deal. Now, you need to find a buyer.

However, when you are starting out for the first time in the wholesale business of real estate, you might not have a list of buyers on hand. But you have to adhere to the settlement within the contracted date as stipulated in the assignment of contract. In such a situation, searching for a first-time buyer would not be your option. Instead, you can seek the help of an investor or contractor who will agree to buy and repair the property. For this purpose, you can seek assistance from the real estate wholesale and investment groups, which you should have joined and stayed in contact with.

Regardless of how you settle your first wholesale deal, if you want to maintain a wholesale real estate business, you must have a buyer's listing which is up-to-date and ready to go. You can search for buyers in different ways, as the other wholesalers do. Keeping the cost of searching the buyers in mind, you can find them in the following ways:

- Advertise the property available for wholesale on some free commercial websites like Craigslist, Zillow, etc.
- Distribute advertising flyers, putting therein the details of the property to be sold with the name and contact number of the contact person.
- Email those investors and contractors whom you have met through the network of wholesalers and investors of real estate, with the details of the property.

Once you begin to receive calls from buyers asking about the property, you must note down their names and contact numbers and create a database of the buyers. Even if those buyers might not show interest in buying the property, you should still keep their basic information and ask them about the type of home they need. I will reiterate this again. Whenever you get a new house property to wholesale, you must add all the buyers' details, even if they are not showing interest in buying that property. This information will increase your database of buyers who can help you in the future. This will also reduce your advertisement cost in the future. When you see that the buyers' list is increasing, you can then use a customer relationship management (CRM) software to provide a better service to your customers.

Negotiate the Deal With a Buyer

As soon as you get a prospective buyer, it is time to negotiate a deal with him or her. Typically, negotiation of a deal is critical because the discussion aiming to reach an agreement involves how much money you can earn from the deal. Your profit is the difference between the value of the property you have purchased and the value of the property you are willing to wholesale for.

As you negotiate the deal with a buyer, you can take advantage of showing the estimate of your contractor to the buyer. You should remember that time is the most important issue in closing a property deal in real estate wholesaling. So, let your buyer know that the deal has to be completed within the stipulated time, as mentioned in the assignment of the contract, if he or she is willing to buy the property. The buyer, with whom you are discussing the deal, should also know that you have other willing buyers who can complete the deal within the scheduled timeframe. You should make sure that the following costs, as well as your profit, are duly covered in the deal price:

- Appraiser fee
- Title searching fee, if you have paid it
- Contractor's/estimator's fee
- Marketing fee, if any
- Your profit from the deal

Generally, the wholesaler of the real estate property aims to earn a minimum profit of $2,000 from a single deal. Aiming to earn a profit below that amount is not a worthy deal, according to the market standard. So, you should be cautious when you fix the deal price with your buyer.

Close the Deal

Once your buyer agrees to buy the property, choose a date for the deal within the date specified in the assignment of contract. All the concerned parties, i.e., both seller and buyer, will go to the office of the title company, and the settlement will be completed there. Unless otherwise stated, the closing costs will be paid by the buyer and seller. After the completion of the settlement, the title of the deed will be transferred in the name of the buyer, and the new owner will get the key of the property.

However, you should prefer an investor-friendly title company because such companies can satisfyingly close the property deal for all the parties involved. According to the assignment clause of the contract, a wholesaler does not generally transfer the property into his or her name. An investor keeps the property in the name of his or her company and avoids the payment of two transfer taxes for two separate transactions.

Chapter 4: Example of Wholesaling With Calculations

Calculating the price of a house property is simple arithmetic. The calculation part will be discussed at the end of this chapter. But first, let's discuss the factors that influence the price of a real estate property.

The value of a real estate property depends on its comparable or in short "comps." It is a property appraisal term that refers to the properties sold recently, concerning the same characteristics or a set of comparable factors. Here, you will get to know the comparable that decides the value of a house property.

1. **Recently Sold Property Listing**: The best way to figure out recently sold property listings is to follow the real estate sites like Zillow, Redfin, etc. Put your preferred city location on the site to explore the recently sold houses by neighborhood on the map. This will enable you to know the number of bedrooms in the house and its price in the same neighborhood. You can further know the square feet, landscape, photos of the rooms, and additional home location information. You can also refine your filter by searching for schools in the area, criminal records in the neighborhood, amenities available in the area, etc. Dividing

the price of the house by the total square feet of the area of the property, will get you an average idea of per square feet rate in that neighborhood.

2. **Similar Property**: Once you get an overall idea from the recently sold houses, searching homes that are nearly the same size, including the same number of rooms, bathrooms, kitchen, and living area with a floor plan that fits your choice may be an easier job. Remember that the comparison must be made in the same neighborhood.

3. **Visit the Home and Compare**: A physical verification of the property is a must to compare it with the information and photo of the rooms and property that you have gotten from the real estate site. This will enable you to make sure that the property and its surroundings are maintained properly. Check the following issues relating to the location of the property:

    - Check if the house is in a quiet neighborhood or on a busy road. The quiet neighborhood would be an advantage for most dwelling.
    - Check if there is proximity to different domestic services and entertainment areas.
    - Check how far the shopping areas and restaurants are from the property.
    - Check if the property is near a toxic site or a landfill. These things are some of

the cons which potential buyers will shy away from.

After getting all the information discussed above, you can now calculate the price of the property. The rule of 70% is the primary basis for calculating to quickly determine the maximum price of the property that you can offer a buyer. For better understanding, let's take an example.

After repair value (ARV) of house property of 1,000 square feet: $300,000

Maximum price of the property is 70% of ARV: $210,000

Less: Renovation estimate: $35,000

Maximum Allowable Offer (MAO): $175,000

Less: Wholesaler's profit (for example): $30,000

Maximum price as a wholesaler that you can offer: $145,000

Per square feet rate as a wholesaler: $145

Chapter 5: How to Find Cash Buyers for Your Deal

Cash buyers help to strengthen the wholesaling business by increasing the flexibility of the transaction. There are many ways to find cash buyers for wholesaling. When the buyers depend on a loan, the process will generally need a detailed inspection of the property in advance, and it may take a week or month to sanction a loan from a bank or finance company. Sometimes, they can reject the application of the buyer to get a loan after the inspection of the property. But, when you choose a cash buyer, you will not have to face these situations.

Generally, corporations, trusts, or funds are cash buyers. But, wholesaler likes to make a deal with an individual cash buyer. The number of individual cash buyers is always going to be small since most buyers will have to earn or save a large amount of money to purchase a real estate property. Sometimes, an heir of an estate can acquire money from winning a lottery, or a person may gain beneficiaries from a settlement. If these two types of buyers are interested in purchasing a real estate property, they may do so in cash. Sometimes, a retired person may be interested in being a cash buyer when he or she gets enough money after retirement. It is essential to find cash buyers for a deal within your real estate wholesaling business. Some of the ways to find cash buyers are as follows.

Use an Online Marketing Tool

You will be open to many more opportunities when using online marketing tools to find cash buyers. You will have to learn, experiment with, and invest some money to use an online marketing tool. But, it will be cheaper than using newspaper advertisements. You can also create a website based on your real estate wholesaling business, as well as social media accounts to give your business more visibility, blog writing, and Google advertisements. If you want to continue your wholesaling business consistently, all of these are advantageous tools to find cash buyers.

Stay With Your Competitors

You cannot avoid your competitors. Instead, you should try to find ways to work together with your competitors. You can bid on your competitor's property at an auction so that you can reach out to them and build a relationship. It will help you to connect with cash buyers for your business.

Get Referrals

There are many agents in wholesaling who have good connections to many of cash buyers. You will try to convey that you are trying to find out cash buyers, and you can help them to fulfill their client's requirements. You agree to offer them a fee for giving you referrals of cash buyers.

Create a List of Cash Buyers

Currently, you can create a targeted list of cash buyers by using todays technological tools. After making a list of selected buyers, you can call, send an e-mail, or use Facebook messenger to contact them and make a deal with cash.

Join a Real Estate Club

You can join a real estate club or a landowners' organization that is near your location. You can spread the information by having conversations with the members. Tell them that you are involved in a wholesaling business, and you are looking for cash buyers. It will help you get cash buyers a lot easier. The more members you meet, the bigger the chance to get cash buyers for your wholesaling business.

Google AdWords

You can use this advertising network to run PPC (pay per click) ads by utilizing. It is one of the more newer ways to get results faster. It will also help to find your main competitors within the wholesaling business. You have to build your website properly, if you want to keep your position at the top of the search results. You will also have to create relevant content focused on search terms that cash buyers would look for online which will boost your ranking within the search engine result page. More viewers will be interested in getting your services, and you will also get more cash buyers.

MLS (Multiple Listing Service)

If you follow the right marketing strategy, you will be able to get cash buyers for your business. By following the MLS, you can get an idea about buyers and what their requirements are regarding real estate properties. You can contact them by providing detailed information about your business. You can expand your list of cash buyers if you can provide them the services according to their requirements.

Check Craigslist

In the section of "houses and apartments for rent" on Craigslist, there sometimes is one person who offers to rent multiple houses, buildings, and lands which he or she owns. These owners have a huge amount of liquid cash, and they purchase different properties solely for renting them out. They also could make great cash buyers.

Follow Public Records

You can search public records where you can check the purchase history of properties. You can also get information about buyers who have purchased properties without taking out any loan from the bank or other financial institutions. You can contact them if you do a little due diligence and find out their contact information.

Keep in Contact With Hard Money Lenders

Sometimes, hard money lenders help cash buyers by lending money to them. So, if you keep in contact with hard money lenders, you will get information about cash buyers. You can contact those cash buyers to sell your real estate property.

If you sell your real estate property to cash buyers, you can complete the transaction procedure in an easy and fast way. You will not have to wait to get your profit, and you also do not have to face any setbacks or hassles with a bank or credit union. You will not experience the hassle of repairing the property when you transact with a cash buyer. Keep in mind that your company's reputation plays an important role when you are looking for cash buyers. If they observe any negative reviews about your wholesaling business, they might refuse to purchase your property.

Chapter 6: How to Maximize Your Profits in Real Estate Wholesaling

You do not have to invest money to start wholesaling. If you work on acquiring knowledge for your real estate market and the skills for crucial negotiation, then you will be able to work confidently and skillfully in the wholesaling business. You can make your profits in real estate wholesaling if you can properly identify a real estate property to sell, considering the market value. Moreover, you can maximize your profits or income if you pay attention to some of the following important factors.

Think About the Seller

If you want to follow the strategies of wholesaling properly, you will have to know how your seller thinks. When the seller eagerly wants to sell his or her property, the seller is called motivated, which plays an important role in the wholesaling business. There are several reasons a seller could be motivated to sell his or her property. A sudden job loss, moving to a different state, and settlement of divorce are common reasons for eagerly trying to sell real estate property. Sometimes, the seller has inherited property after the death of his or her close relative, or the seller wants to get relief from taking care of other people's properties by selling it. Irrespective of the reason, understanding the motivation of the seller is essential to maximize your profits in real estate.

A smooth transaction with a seller is what all wholesalers want. Here are some questions to ask yourself whenever you deal with sellers:

- **How will you impress a seller to trust and depend on you?** If you want to potentially impress a seller to depend on you, you will have to be personable and someone that the seller could relate to. Aside from making great conversations, you should be able to support them to overcome stress or personal issues related to the sale of their property.

- **In what types of situations would a seller think of selling his or her property?** When a seller eagerly wants to sell his or her property, there must be a reason that pushes him or her to sell the property. You will have to understand the actual situation to create an opportunity for a smooth transaction.

- **How can a seller contact you as a reliable figure in the wholesaling business?** When you identify a seller of a property, you can give out your contact number, e-mail address. It's always good to have business cards with you which also contain your website address, which sellers can contact you at. It will help a seller to communicate with you much easier.

- **How did the seller maintain his or her property during the previous years?** The maintenance and upkeep of the property during previous years plays an important role in pricing the property according to the market value.

Maintain Transparency

You will have to maintain ethics and transparency if you want to be successful in your wholesaling business.

By following some principles, you can maintain transparency to maximize your profit in the wholesaling business.

- You will have to present yourself as a principal buyer to the seller of the real estate property and also as a principal seller to the buyer, considering each part of the transaction.
- You must use a valid written agreement of purchasing and selling the property while conforming to the requirements of the local market.
- You should represent yourself as a contract holder for handling all marketing materials. Your agreement will disclose your position clearly within the transaction of the real estate property.
- You will have to establish yourself as a licensed agent of wholesaling business when you agree with a seller or buyer of the property.
- Your action related to the wholesaling business should be ethical, appropriate, and on time so that the seller and buyer will not have any doubts about your transparency.

- If you want to confirm a wholesale deal, you can take the initiative and deposit some money. It will help to establish the validity of your impending transaction for the real estate property. Moreover, it will develop your importance to the seller, and he or she will eagerly try to make an agreement with you for the property.
- While establishing an agreement with the seller, you should think about a backup plan. It will help to maintain your transparency within the wholesaling business.
- You will have to explain clearly to the buyer that you are not the owner of the property, but you are selling the right to buy the property.

Build Your Exit Strategy

There are many reasons for building an exit strategy for those who are in the wholesaling business. This strategy is a means to curb losses and manage risks; it may also help to maintain your profit in the business. The importance of building an exit strategy is detailed as follows.

- Developing an exit strategy allows you to take an action plan and reduce the forthcoming risks. By evaluating the potential exit strategies before making an agreement with the seller, you will understand the risks you are taking and also be able to avoid them.
- Thinking about an exit strategy is essential in being successful in real estate wholesaling. Before making an agreement with a seller for

wholesaling his or her property, you need to keep a clear idea of how to profit from the property when you decide to exit from the deal.

- Sometimes, after agreeing with a seller or a buyer, you may find that the wholesale is not suitable for you. Or sometimes, you might have issues in adjusting to the wholesale agreement which you notice has become a burden to you. You should always have an exit strategy before entering a wholesale agreement.

Ensure Good Communication Skills

Good communication skills are essential in every workplace. You have to develop an essential attitude toward ensuring good communication. If you can communicate effectively, it will convey your message to another person unambiguously and properly. When you are involved in real estate wholesaling, your inadequate skill for communication can create misunderstandings. It will reduce profitability, sales, and chances of closing a transaction. There are important factors that can ensure your good communication skills, and these are as follows.

- Powerful listening skill: Your powerful listening skills are advantageous in any business deals. This allows you to include other people's views when striking the deal. You also learn new concepts by improving your listening skills.
- Writing efficiency: Your writing efficiency will help you to be informative. You can focus on the important things in order to communicate

effectively with the people involved in wholesaling.

- Efficient presentation: Your efficient presentation of ideas and information to the audience will inspire them to engage in your business. They will be effectively motivated, and you can communicate with them easily to increase the rate at which you close your business deals.
- Maintain good relationships: When you agree with a real estate seller, he or she will want to get feedback regarding the progression of the deal. Buyers will also show their interest in new properties you are working on. So, you will have to maintain good relations and keep in contact with them regularly to ensure good communication. A good relationship creates an opportunity to get more business in the future.

Don't Forget Follow-Up Strategy

Finding new sellers, as well as buyers, is important to continue wholesaling. If you communicate with your previous buyers to get their opinion on whether they are satisfied with how you handled the sale of the property, it may be a good follow-up strategy for your wholesaling business. If they are satisfied, you can ask them whether they have any plans to purchase another real estate property, or if they know anyone who would like to purchase a property. Getting referrals of buyers from them is a good way to expand your client base.

On the other hand, you can try to help them if they have any issues with the real estate property that they have purchased from you. When they are satisfied with your services, they might inspire others to contact you for selling or purchasing real estate property. It will boost your wholesaling business. You will also get more opportunities to maximize your profit in your wholesaling business.

When you agree upon the purchasing and selling of real estate property, you should include different important terms in the contract, and these important terms are as follows.

- Make a list of parties involved in the wholesaling business.
- Include detailed information of the real estate property.
- Mention about adding any personal property within the sale.
- Explain clearly the purchase price and the option of financing.
- Discus the financial terms and plan of contingency.
- Include a plan of contingency.
- Confirm the physical real estate property when the transaction is made.
- Decide on the deadline for the closing date.
- Discuss the type of deed.
- Include state-specific adjustments, such as sewage, taxes, water, and so on.
- Include a statement of damage and risk.
- Present a default clause of the buyer, as well as the seller.

Chapter 7: Step-by-Step Process on How to Close a Wholesaling Deal

Presently, a wholesaler follows two ways to make a profit from real estate wholesaling. One of these two ways is the assignment of a contract, and another is double closing. It is important to understand the differences between these two methods of wholesaling to achieve your goal in real estate wholesaling.

What Is an Assignment of Contract?

An assignment of a contract is an important tool for a wholesaler. When a seller of a real estate property agrees to assign an agreement to an agent of the wholesaling business, the wholesaler holds the right to buy the property, and he or she also uses the right to sell that property to a buyer. A wholesaler sells an agreement that he or she has made with the owner of the real estate property. This type of assignment of contract is usually the first option of a wholesaler. It is the easiest method to enter into a wholesaling business without investing any amount of money. An assignment of contract must explain clearly the profits that an agent of the wholesaling business and the seller might expect from the deal. You will explain the basics of the wholesaling business within the contract. You will not make it complicated to scare away the seller. When you make a contract for the sale of the property, there are essential things that a seller needs to know. These are:

- You are not purchasing the real estate property, and you are working as a wholesaler.
- Anyone else can purchase it outright.
- If he or she has failed to find a suitable buyer to purchase the property, the contract will be canceled.
- The seller needs to know about the progress of the sale.

What Is Double Closing?

A double closing is considered as a side-by-side closing. A wholesaler will buy a real estate property just for reselling it as soon as possible without rehabbing it. The double closing procedure can be completed within a few hours or a few weeks. Indeed, double closings are different from traditional purchasing and selling, as they are followed through at a faster pace.

The double closing procedure involves two transactions. The first transaction is made between the seller of the real estate property and the agent of the wholesaling business. The second transaction is made between the agent of the wholesaling business and the new purchaser of real estate property. Two transactions are independent, and settlement statements, as well as escrow, are used to fulfill their specific purposes. The success of double closing depends on timing. When you decide on the double closing process, you will have to take the risk as you have no control over the transaction. It is very important to think about cash buyers before following a double closing procedure. Having a list of eager cash buyers in advance helps to follow a double closing procedure of real estate property smoothly.

5 Steps to Double Closing

Generally, a real estate agent chooses double closing as the second option for the deal. The double closing procedure involves two independent transactions that require costs separately. On the other hand, when an agent purchases real estate property from the seller, he or she will have to invest money. This can be profitable when the wholesaler knows where he or she can sell the real estate property that he or she has already purchased from the seller. Cash buyers play an important role in the double closing procedure of the wholesaling business. Sometimes, banks or financial companies disqualify real estate properties for a traditional mortgage or loan. This is where cash buyers play an important role in helping to speed up the wholesaling process. If you want to follow the double closing procedure in making a deal in wholesaling, then you should follow these five simple steps:

1. Put in effort to find a seller: When an agent of real estate wholesaling purchases a real estate property from a seller, the agent will try to find a property suitable for the deal. The agent will try to find a property that is available at a discount or at an attractive price to resell it. It will help the agent to make a good profit at the time of the second transaction. As the agent,

you need to create a budget for the property that you will buy to address any issues.

2. Run the numbers: Real estate agents such as yourself must be deeply knowledgeable of the numbers involved in the business. By showing the calculated numbers, you can expose the other parties to the opportunity of making a profit so that they will be interested in purchasing the property.

3. Find buyers in advance: When you make the first transaction of the double closing method, you should try to find buyers in advance. If you make a list of buyers who are interested in purchasing a real estate property, it will help you with the second transaction of double closing easily and quickly. If the new buyer wants to take a loan to purchase the real estate property, it will be advantageous to you because it ensures the eligibility of the second transaction.

4. Purchase the real estate property from the original owner: You should purchase the real estate property from the original owner of the real estate property in a normal transaction by paying the closing costs. You will take the settlement statement for the first transaction.

5. Sell the property to the new purchaser: Lastly, you make the second transaction to complete the deal. You will consider it just like a normal sale of a property. You also take another settlement statement by paying the usual costs.

Chapter 8: Tips for a Successful Real Estate Wholesaling Business

At first, real estate wholesaling might seem easy for you but later on you might even find yourself struggling to make profits. This is because you are not following the right strategies. Usually, it is the novice investor who is attracted to investing in wholesaling, but you will gradually realize that it takes quite a comprehensive knowledge of the market to make considerable profits here. So, here are some tips that will give you a boost toward being successful in real estate wholesaling.

Train Your Mindset

Having the right mindset is important for every entrepreneur, whether it is in the real estate business or anywhere else. Your mindset is what makes you successful. Also, the right mindset is not something you gain overnight. You have to give it time and cultivate it. But once you have acquired the right mindset, nothing can stop you, and you will become more dedicated than ever. Also, if you want to be consistent, then having the right mindset is necessary.

For developing the right mindset, one of the first things that you have to do is deal with self-doubt and fear in your mind. Fear will not help you in any way, whatsoever, and it will only hold you back. Also, what you see on the surface might be only the tip of the iceberg. If you want to know things in detail, you will have to dig deeper. You should also think about the worst that can happen because, at times, thinking about the worst-case scenarios can boost your positivity, because you are able to properly prepare for an less than stella outcome.

Make Proper Use of Technology

If you make the best use of the technology available today, then you can go a lot further than those who don't. Your workflow will become more organized, and everything will function in a more accurate manner. There are so many tools that you can use and automate some of the functions that you don't necessarily have to do yourself. Also, you should not forget how crucial the role of marketing is, even in wholesale real estate. The wider the area you cover, the more chances you have of getting better deals. Reaching a bigger audience has now become easier and more strategic with the help of digital marketing, and you should make complete use of it.

Also, targeting your audience through social media is something you can do by implementing the right tools. In the business of wholesalers, the majority of your audience will be taxpayers, absentee owners, and also homeowners in pre-foreclosure. So, with social media like Facebook or Instagram, you can set your target audience and develop an effective marketing campaign that will bring you the right audience.

Design an Effective Website

Having an attractive website as a real estate wholesaler can be a complete game-changer. Making profits in wholesaling depends on how quickly you can come up with a prospective buyer's list. Well, it is not really any secret how having a website can really help you out in any business, and the facts are the same for real estate wholesaling. What is the first thought you have when you visit a person's website? You would hope to think that they are credible, don't you? Well, similarly, when someone visits your website, they will think that you are a wholesaler who can be trusted if your website is professionally created.

Also, when you have a website, building your cash buyer's list will become easier than ever before. You can keep opt-in forms on your website, which they can use to enter in their contact information. Another advantage of having a website is allowing you to send push notifications to your clients whenever you have a deal in your hand. This will help you to grab the attention of your potential buyers instead of an email that can get lost in their inbox. When you have a website, you can also show the properties that you have sold. By doing this, you can make your audience see that you are the real deal and build some credibility.

Make Use of Real Estate Neighborhood Comps

This is an important point that wholesalers often overlook. If you fail to identify the potential comp home sales, then you will never be able to make good profits in real estate wholesaling. This will also help you set competitive prices. There is another advantage to having access to the neighborhood comps. That is, you will know which properties in your neighborhood are being sold for a price that is below the market. The key to attracting buyers is offering the right price, and having the neighborhood comps will help you in the process.

Have a Proper Understanding of the Market

The market is truly everything when it comes to real estate wholesaling. Now, as a beginner, you might think you know what is going on right now, but can you predict what will happen in a couple of years? If not, then you need some brushing up and gain a better understanding of the market. Getting the right neighborhood is so important. Getting a contract for a house in the wrong neighborhood might land you with a house that no one wants to buy, no matter how good the house is. You should also understand that rental property investors are the ones who will be your most reliable buyers. So, you need to figure out the neighborhoods that have a strong rental market.

Also, there are three major factors that you should keep in mind in order to understand the market properly. The first is employment. When there is an increase in employment in a neighborhood, people will automatically be looking for properties there. On the other hand, if a neighborhood has incidents like factory closures, massive layoffs, or outsourcing, then the jobs will decrease, and so will the demand for new properties. The second factor to keep in mind is the supply. Here, supply means the total number of houses that are available for sale, and you should check this based on a fixed time scale, say six months, which is considered to be a healthy market time span. If the number of houses is less, then the demand will possibly be more, and the prices will rise accordingly. The third factor is affordability. The local market will also be influenced by the affordability of people. There might be some really good houses, but if the people could not afford it, you either have to look for buyers in other places or change your locality altogether.

Know Your Buyers

Just as you need to have proper knowledge of the market, you also need to know your buyers if you want to be successful in your real estate wholesaling endeavor. You need to understand the type or style of home that your investor is looking for. And for this, you need to cultivate a positive relationship with your buyers, get to know them, and ask for the information you need to cater to them in the best way possible. If you are working with rental property investors, know the type of neighborhood they are looking for. Remember that not everyone is looking for the same thing, so you must not make any assumptions.

The best way to know your buyers is to build a database where you can keep all this information stored. This will also assist you in the case of recurring buyers. Your buyers will also be pleased that they have approached someone who already knows what they want. This will, in turn, help you build long-term relationships and proper contacts in the real estate market.

Use CRM Software

Sometimes, you need to know when you need to delegate some of your tasks so that you can focus on the tasks that you are better at doing. Keeping track of all your clients can be a cumbersome task if you plan to do it manually. But in today's world of automation, there are lots of CRM or Customer Relationship Management software that can help you out. An old-school spreadsheet won't suffice for the task of tracking down all your clients and leads. With CRM software, you can segregate the buyers, keep track of all property information, constantly update your growing database of contacts, and stay at the top of your game.

There are loads of CRM software in the market that you can use, and all of them have their own pros and cons. So, you need to make a comparative study of all of them before finalizing one for your needs. First, you need to ask yourself what value that particular CRM software will give your business. You also need to jot down the features you are looking for and check it against the software in question. You also need to keep a fixed budget for your software.

These are only some of the points that you should keep in mind if you want to be successful and make some good profits in real estate wholesaling.

Conclusion

Thank you for making it through the end of *Wholesaling: A Beginner's Guide to Wholesale Real Estate*. It was a very informative journey and I was able to provide you with all of the tools you need to achieve your goals in wholesaling.

The next step is to implement the various things that you have learned. When it comes to the arena of real estate, wholesaling definitely offers you a great earning opportunity, but only if you are ready to take it. Requiring almost no capital at all, wholesaling allows you to get the hang of what the real estate market is like. Also, don't let the fear of rejection hold you back. Sometimes, people shy away from it simply because they feel that the needs of their lead buyers won't be met by their offer. But you will never know if you don't make the offer in the first place.

You have to remember that the success you get will depends on the number of offers you make and not the rejections you get. Lastly, there is nothing to lose here. So, why not give it a shot? You might end up making a hefty profit the next day; you never know! Spend time in building your network because that is crucial in becoming successful at wholesaling. Talk to the people you meet because you never know who might be your next potential seller or buyer. You might not get the imagined profit at first, but you have to be patient. Perseverance is the key to success.

Thank You

I would like to thank you from the bottom of my heart for coming along with me on this wholesaling real estate journey. There are many real estate books out there, but you decided to give this one a chance.

If you liked this book, then I need your help!

Please take a moment to leave an honest review for this book. This feedback gives me a good understanding of the kinds of books and topics readers want to read about and it will also give my book more visibility.

Leaving a review takes less than one minute and is much appreciated.

www.ingramcontent.com/pod-product-compliance
Lightning Source LLC
Chambersburg PA
CBHW071520210326
41597CB00018B/2825